NEVE
THE PEACOCKS
The Ultimate
LEEDS UNITED
QUIZ BOOK

ANITA CLARK

The History Press

For my much-loved gran, Gwen Schofield,
who raised an army of Leeds United fans
and was fiercely proud of us all.

First published 2013

The History Press
The Mill, Brimscombe Port
Stroud, Gloucestershire, GL5 2QG
www.thehistorypress.co.uk

Reprinted 2015

British Library Cataloguing in Publication Data.
A catalogue record for this book is available from the British Library.

ISBN 978 0 7524 9880 5

Typesetting and origination by The History Press
Printed in Great Britain

Contents

	Foreword	5
	Acknowledgements	7
	Introduction	8
Round 1	Premier Leeds	10
Round 2	All the Glory of the Cup	13
Round 3	The Boss	16
Round 4	It's all Relative!	19
Round 5	Leeds International	22
Round 6	'White' from the Start	25
Round 7	Away Days	28
Round 8	War of the Roses	30
Round 9	Name that Player	33
Round 10	We was Robbed	39
Round 11	It'll be all 'White' on the Night	42
Round 12	The Last is the First	45
Round 13	Leeds! Leeds! Leeds!	48
Round 14	Hot Shots	51
Round 15	Super Stoppers	54
Round 16	Three Lions on a Shirt	57

Round 17	What's in a Name?	60
Round 18	We've had our Ups and Downs…	63
Round 19	The 'Other' Cup	67
Round 20	White Hot Debuts	70
Round 21	Connect Four	74
Round 22	Sergeant Wilko's Barmy Army	79
Round 23	The Price is 'White'	82
Round 24	The Life and Times of Leeds United	85
Round 25	We are the Champions, Champions of Europe!	87
Round 26	'Managing to Succeed'	90
Round 27	Who Scored the Goal?	93
Round 28	The Kids are all 'White'	95
Round 29	Sweet Charity	98
Round 30	Marching on Together	101
	The Answers	105

Foreword

by Dominic Matteo
(Leeds United 2000–2004)

It was a great pleasure to be asked to write the foreword for this book as I have a huge affection for both Leeds United and the club's supporters. I thoroughly enjoyed my spell as a player at Elland Road and have some fantastic memories of my football-playing days in West Yorkshire.

It couldn't have begun much better for me, as I made my debut in the legendary 1–0 Champions League victory over Italian giants AC Milan at Elland Road in September 2000. Not a bad way to start your career with a new club!

In fact, the whole of my first season at Leeds was packed with memorable moments; and none more so than our trip to the San Siro. To be involved in such a game was fantastic, but then to score the goal that secured our progression to the second group stage of the Champions League was an extra special moment that I will treasure for the rest of my life.

Although our European adventure ultimately ended in semi-final agony in Valencia, it was fantastic to be part of a team that put Leeds firmly back on the European map. We also enjoyed success in the Premier League that season too, finishing fourth and securing UEFA Cup qualification for the following campaign.

My four seasons with Leeds were a fantastic time for me and I feel privileged not only to have played football for such a great club, but also to have had the ultimate honour of wearing the captain's armband. I look back with immense pride at the time

I spent at Leeds United and, even though it did eventually end in relegation heartache, I do have many wonderful memories of my time at Elland Road and I am extremely proud to be associated so strongly with such a distinguished club.

This superb little quiz book has certainly fetched back some of those great memories for me and I've also learnt a thing or two about the club too. I'm sure all Leeds fans will enjoy testing their knowledge of the club and grappling with the questions – no doubt great memories will come flooding back for you as well.

All the very best to all Leeds United fans,

Dom

Since retiring from football, Dom has become involved in an array of activities. He is a Football Ambassador for Leeds United FC, and he owns the Rock Bar in Leeds city centre. He is also very popular on both the after-dinner speaking and corporate engagement circuits, and can be contacted via info@dominicmatteo.co.uk.

Acknowledgements

The generous help and support of many people has been invaluable during the writing of this book. Firstly, I would like to thank Tony Schofield, Paul Schofield, John Schofield and Steve Willshaw for painstakingly working through all of the questions, offering their opinions and allowing me to pick their brains.

Thanks also to Jean Sutherland for the loan of her fabulous collection of Leeds United tickets from the Revie era, and also to Fred Watson for very kindly loaning me his collection of programmes dating back to the 1960s. Samples from both collections, along with my own, have been reprinted in this book.

I'd also like to thank Dominic Matteo for being kind enough to supply the foreword for the book, and Leeds United Football Club for all of their help and support.

Finally, I want to offer a big thank you to Andrew, Elinor and Daniel for all of their love, patience and support.

All images have been reproduced with the kind permission of Leeds United Football Club.

Introduction

Welcome to *The Ultimate Leeds United Quiz Book*, a light-hearted but informative book designed primarily to entertain. The book is structured into thirty themed rounds of eleven questions, with an extra 'teaser' at the end of each round for you to puzzle over.

Many of the questions in this book have been born from the anecdotes passed down through my family. As part of a large family of Leeds United fans, I grew up listening to recounts of past glories – I have known the names of Bremner, Lorimer, Hunter and Gray almost as long as I have known my own!

Over fifty years of experiences following Leeds United home and away reverberate around my family and we have been represented at most of the iconic, highly significant moments in the club's history. Over the past quarter of a century I have added my own highs and lows to that family narrative.

Although I have referenced these memories, recounts and experiences when writing the book, I have backed this up with exhaustive research to corroborate all of the facts and figures contained in the questions and answers. I have meticulously checked every detail, using a variety of sources including programmes, books and the internet.

However, I am only human; it is possible that a minor error or anomaly may have avoided detection and been inadvertently left to masquerade as fact in the book. If you therefore think, for example, that I have misquoted the transfer fee paid for a particular player, I can only apologise and hope that this does not spoil your enjoyment of the book – although, of course, it may be your source that is unreliable!

In addition, over time some of the answers to questions in the book will inevitably change. For instance, I'm assuming I'll be on safe ground for some time yet with the last Leeds United player to score for the full England team – but you never know! Therefore, all I can say is that the information in the book was correct and up to date as of August 2013.

There are no fixed rules about how to use the book: you can read it on your own or with your mates, in competition or as part of a team. It is entirely up to you! Whatever you do and however you complete the questions, though, I hope you enjoy reading the book as much as I have enjoyed writing it.

Anita Clark, 2013

Round 1

Premier Leeds

Although it may be hard for many of today's youngsters to believe, Leeds United was actually a founder member of the FA Premier League. And we weren't just making up the numbers either – in the Premier League's first season we were actually the reigning top-tier Champions. While we never quite emulated that success in any of our Premier League campaigns, we did have long spells in that League when we weren't half bad! So let's indulge ourselves with a look back over one of the golden eras in our club's history – the Premier League years.

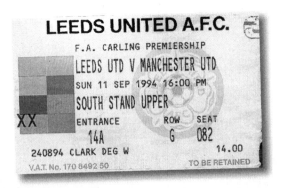

1   How many seasons in total did we spend in the Premier League?

2   Can you name the striker who scored our first Premier League goal in the 2–1 home victory over Wimbledon and ended the season as the club's top scorer?

3   The Premier League's very first hat-trick was scored by a Leeds United player. Which enigmatic marksman netted 3 of the goals in our 5–0 victory over Spurs in August 1992?

4   And can you name the striker who scored the most League goals in total for us during our time in the Premier League?

5   What unwanted record did we set on our travels during our inaugural season in the Premier League?

6   Who was our club captain during that first campaign?

7   And can you recall who captained the team with distinction in our final Premier League season?

8   Eddie Gray was in charge of our last game in the Premier League, and Howard Wilkinson had been the manager in the very first. But can you name the four men who occupied the managerial hot seat in the intervening years?

9   And which long-serving full-back made the most
    Premier League appearances in a Leeds shirt?

10 Our highest Premier League finish was achieved in the
    1999/2000 season. In which lofty position did we finish?

11 And finally, defeat against which team in May 2004
    signalled the end of our time in the Premier League?

FACT OR FICTION?

*Jonathan Woodgate made more Premier
League appearances for Leeds than David
Wetherall.*

All the Glory
of the Cup

The FA Cup, first contested when Queen Victoria was on the throne, retains a special place in the hearts of all English football fans. It is steeped in history, legend and folklore. And Leeds United's involvement in the FA Cup has enriched the competition and produced many nail-biting moments and stomach-churning ups and downs for the club's supporters! So step onto the FA Cup rollercoaster and see what you can recall about our triumphs and tribulations, 'giant killings', shock defeats, extra-time agonies, replays, more replays, semi-final heartbreaks, final-day woes and celebrations!

1 Let's start with the obvious question: in which year did we win the FA Cup for the only time in our history, and who scored the winning goal?

2 In total, how many times have Leeds United reached the FA Cup final?

3   Which midfield dynamo headed a late winner in the
    1965 FA Cup semi-final replay against Man United
    to book our first ever
    Wembley appearance?

4   And which skilful winger
    and Elland Road favourite
    made history in 1965
    when he became the first
    black player to appear in
    an FA Cup final?

5   In the 2007/08 season,
    Leeds suffered a shock
    first-round exit from
    the FA Cup. Can you
    name the Second
    Division opponents
    who prevailed with a 1–0 victory at Elland Road?

6   And in 2012/13, which Premier League team did we
    knock out of the FA Cup?

7   What was remarkable about Leeds United's record in
    the FA Cup between 1952/53 and 1961/62?

8   In 1990/91, Leeds were involved in a marathon fourth-
    round FA Cup tie. Who eventually overcame us in the
    third replay, with a 2–1 victory at Elland Road?

9   And who were our opponents in an epic four-game FA Cup quarter-final during the 1974/75 campaign?

10 In 1987, we reached the FA Cup semi-final while challenging for promotion from the Second Division. Who captained the team in that semi-final, which ultimately finished in extra-time disappointment?

11 And finally, which Leeds United FA Cup game is sixth on the list of the UK's 'most watched TV programmes of all time'?

FACT OR FICTION?

The team Leeds have been drawn against most often in the FA Cup is Man United.

The Boss

This quiz book just had to include a round devoted to the late, great Don Revie – one of Elland Road's all-time heroes. His name is synonymous with Leeds United and his managerial genius sparked the most explosively successful period in the club's history. Revie was a real thinker of the game, a master tactician producing detailed dossiers on opposing teams. He also worked hard to foster a family atmosphere at Elland Road, enjoying cosy pre-match games of bingo with his players! So here we go with eleven questions about our most celebrated manager – dabbers at the ready and eyes down for a full house!

1 Don Revie is obviously iconic as a manager at Elland Road, but he actually made 80 appearances as a player for Leeds United. In which year did he become a Leeds player, and from which club was he signed?

2 In 1955, Revie won which prestigious footballing award?

3 Prior to accepting the Leeds job, Revie was offered
the managerial hot-seat at a lower-league south-coast
club. Can you name the club that almost pinched
him from us?

4 Revie famously changed the Leeds United kit from blue
and gold to all-white, the colours of Real Madrid. At the
start of which season did this defining change occur?

5 In which season did Revie guide the club to promotion
from the Second Division?

6   Leeds competed in the First Division for 10 of the
    seasons that Revie was in charge, winning the title twice.
    But how many times did we finish runners-up?

7   How many European finals did Leeds reach under
    Don Revie?

8   And how many European and domestic cup
    competitions did the team win during his tenure?

9   Revie inspired fierce loyalty amongst his players, with
    many remaining at Elland Road for over a decade. But
    can you name one of his long-serving unsung heroes
    who, despite not being a first-team regular, showed
    his value when scoring a vital away goal in the 1971
    Inter-Cities Fairs Cup final at Juventus?

10 Who were the opponents in Don Revie's last League
    game as manager of the club?

11 Finally, when Revie left Leeds he recommended to the
    board a successor – one of his own players. Which
    midfield supremo did he suggest for the role?

FIVES AND FOURS

*Five of Revie's 'Aces' were included in the first
PFA Team of the Year in 1973/74. Can you name
them?*

Round

4

It's all Relative!

Don Revie certainly worked hard to foster a 'big family' atmosphere during his time at Elland Road, and Leeds United has always prided itself on being a family club. That strong family orientation has often made it onto the pitch as well, with the Leeds United 'bring a younger relative to work' scheme paying rich dividends over the years! So see how you get on with this round of questions that tests your knowledge of Leeds United's extended footballing family connections.

1 Let's kick off with a 'relatively' easy one: which two brothers played for Leeds in the 1975 European Cup final?

2 Another pair of brothers both moved to Elland Road during the mid-1980s but, although each made over 50 League appearances for the club, they never played together in the same Leeds team. Can you name the two brothers?

3 Which future Elland Road defensive midfielder was
   a ballboy at Wembley for the 1968 League Cup final,
   during which his brother picked up a winner's medal
   when Leeds beat Arsenal?

4 Continuing the League Cup theme: which nephew of a
   member of the Leeds 1968 League Cup final team went
   on to follow in his uncle's footsteps by playing for Leeds
   in the 1996 final?

5 And which Leeds United uncle and nephew combo
   were selected to fill the full-back roles on numerous
   occasions during our Premier League era?

6 Which nephew of Johnny Giles followed in his uncle's footsteps by making 65 League appearances in the Leeds midfield during the 1980s?

7 Jack, George and Jim Milburn were all full-backs who served our club with great distinction across four decades, from the 1920s to the 1950s. But who was their famous nephew who became a legend in the Revie era?

8 Which famous Elland Road striker from the 1970s had four brothers who also all played professional football (although none of them with Leeds United)?

9 A Leeds goalscoring legend from the 1920s and '30s was also a member of a unique family of footballing brothers who scored more than 500 League goals between them. Can you name him?

10 Also, can you recall the names of the twin brothers who arrived at Elland Road from Southampton in 1991?

11 And finally, which set of twins played in the Leeds United Development Squad during the 2012/13 season?

FACT OR FICTION?

During the 1970/71 season, two brothers each scored a goal in the same League fixture at Elland Road.

Leeds
International

Back in the Revie era, the vast majority of players plying their trade in the English Football League hailed from our own shores, and 'overseas' signings tended to consist mainly of those hardy souls who journeyed across the Irish sea from Eire! How times have changed. The English game today abounds with foreign talent, and Leeds United has benefited from the services of some truly magnificent international players. Not all of the club's foreign imports have been runaway successes though, so be warned: this round may feature a couple of dismal signings that you had hoped to forget!

I   Former Leeds captain and recipient of the FIFA Fair Play Award in 2000. The club's most capped player, making 58 appearances for his native South Africa, while at Elland Road.

2   Also hailing from South Africa, this player scored a nine-minute extra-time hat-trick for Leeds in a third round FA Cup replay in 1995.

3   Popular American who joined Leeds from Preston in 2005 and was voted Supporters' Player of the Year in 2006/07. One of two Leeds United players to represent his country in the 2006 World Cup finals.

4   The second of our players to feature in the 2006 World Cup finals. An Angolan defender who made 90 League appearances for the club between 2005 and 2010.

5   Australian centre forward who arrived at Elland Road from Celtic in 2000. He was the last Leeds player to score a hat-trick in the Premier League.

6   Voted both Players' and Supporters' Player of the Year in 2010/11, this tricky winger won his first cap for Ivory Coast while playing at Leeds.

7   Ghanaian hotshot who joined Leeds from Eintracht Frankfurt in 1995. He developed a taste for scoring spectacular goals and also, apparently, for scoffing Yorkshire puddings during his time at Elland Road.

8　Quality French midfielder who added bite to O'Leary's youthful team. This player fell out of favour with the Irishman's successor, Terry Venables, and departed for Roma in 2003.

9　Another O'Leary signing, this young Norwegian midfielder lit up Elland Road following his arrival in 1999 and was voted the club's Young Player of the Year in his first season. However, a succession of injuries ultimately saw his seven-year stint in West Yorkshire end with a bit of a whimper.

10　Here it comes – brace yourself! Tubby Swedish import who, shall we say, didn't exactly live up to the hype at Elland Road following his signing from Parma in 1995.

11　And finally … Brazilian World Cup winner whose time at Leeds is generally not remembered fondly! Dismissed on his home debut after conceding a penalty, this defender's loan stint produced just a single win from 7 appearances and 25 goals conceded.

FIVES AND FOURS

Five players who played in a League fixture for Leeds during the 2012/13 campaign were born outside of Britain and Ireland. Can you name them?

'White'
from
the Start

Rising from the ashes of Leeds City Football Club, it's fair to say that the first forty or so years for Leeds United did not exactly glitter with glory. However, the club's early supporters did, like all subsequent Leeds fans, have their successes to cheer and, inevitably, bitter disappointments to endure. You may not be able to say 'I was there!' but what do you know about those early years at Elland Road?

1   OK, let's start right back at the beginning: in which year was Leeds United AFC formed?

2   Can you name the club's very first manager?

3   And do you know the colours of the first Leeds United kit?

4   A tricky one now to test the real anoraks amongst you!
Our first-ever League fixture was against a team that
was unpopular with early Leeds fans. Who were the
opponents and why were they so disliked?

5   Another tough one: can you name the player who
earned himself a permanent place in the history books
by scoring the club's first ever Football League goal?

6   A slightly more recent one now: which celebrated
player, who made his Leeds debut at the age of 17,
scored 150 League goals in eight years before joining
Juventus in 1957 for a British-record fee at the time?

7   And can you name the legendary skipper who not only
made over 400 club appearances at right half before
retiring in 1943, but was also the first Leeds United
man to play for England?

8   Do you know the name of the Leeds and England
'Iron Man', signed in 1929, who never shaved before a
game to enhance his tough image, although in fact he was
never booked or sent off in his entire footballing career?

9   And which loyal left-back, who played his entire
professional career for Leeds United, made 474
appearances in total between 1948 and 1964?

10 In which season did we win promotion to the top tier of
    English football for the first time?

11 Finally, what was Leeds United's highest League finishing
    position before Don Revie's appointment as manager?

FACT OR FICTION?

Two different birds have featured on
Leeds United's club badge over the years: one
is a peacock and the other is an owl.

BLACKPOOL FOOTBALL CLUB LTD.

FOOTBALL LEAGUE DIVISION 1

BLACKPOOL
V
LEEDS UNITED

Saturday, 13th March
KICK-OFF 3-0 p.m.

A. Mc. Bain.

Secretary

RES. SEAT 11/- or 55p

Issued subject to the Rules, Regulations and
Bye-Laws of the Football Association
and Football League
No Ticket exchanged nor money refunded
THIS PORTION TO BE RETAINED

**WEST
STAND**

SECTION

E

ENTRANCE

2 OR **13**

ROW   SEAT

Q148

Away Days

Leeds United unquestionably enjoys the finest, most loyal away support in the land – not to mention the noisiest! And over the years that vociferous band of travelling supporters has been rewarded with some truly magnificent away performances along, of course, with one or two desperate defeats. So this round is for anyone who's followed Leeds away from home through thick and thin, in sunshine and in rain, to some of the grandest and also, let's face it, some of the most dismal grounds in England and beyond. The venue and date of a Leeds game has been given: correctly identify the opposition and award yourself a point; recall the score and significance of each game and you can officially call yourself a Leeds United genius!

1   St Mary's Stadium, 19 November 2005.
2   Boothferry Park, 28 April 1956.
3   Vetch Field, 11 April 1964.
4   Stadio Olimpico, 5 December 2000.
5   Layer Road, 13 February 1971.
6   The City Ground, 29 November 2011.

7   Filbert Street, 9 October 2001.

8   Hillsborough, 12 April 1987.

9   Camp Nou, 23 April 1975.

10 Bridge Road, 30 November 2008.

11 Selhurst Park, 23 September 1995.

FIVES AND FOURS

Leeds made five trips across the Pennines during the 2012/13 season. Can you name each of the five Lancashire grounds that we visited for first-team fixtures in 2012/13?

WEST TERRACE (HOLGATE)
STANDING
MIDDLESBROUGH v
LEEDS
UNITED
SATURDAY 9TH DEC. 89
KICK-OFF 3.00 P.M.
BARCLAYS LEAGUE TWO

| PRICE (inc. V.A.T.) | This ticket is valid for the match stated either on the due date or later if postponed. It is not valid for a replay of a match started and later abandoned. No cash refund will be given if not used. This ticket is issued subject to the rules and regulations of the Football League and the Football Association. | GATES 70-76 , 80-89 |
| £ 4.00 | | TICKET NO 01962 |

MIDDLESBROUGH F.C.
AYRESOME PARK, MIDDLESBROUGH

TO BE RETAINED

War of
the Roses

When asked to list their sworn deadly enemies, football fans
from other clubs and neutrals alike seem to cite Leeds United
more often than any other. And when it comes to our stated
enemies, it's fair to say we may harbour one or two niggling
grudges of our own! There is one club, however, divided
from us by two-score miles and a hilly wasteland, for which
we reserve our deepest contempt. I know this will be hard,
but try to keep your head as you charge deep into enemy
territory in this latter-day War of the Roses!

1   The first ever clash between Leeds and Man United was
    a Second Division encounter in January 1923: what was
    the final score?

2   On the way to Wembley in 1970, we knocked out our old
    adversaries in the FA Cup semi-final. How many replays
    were required and who eventually scored the deciding goal?

3 And, much more recently, which player's goal sent Man United crashing out of the FA Cup at the third-round stage in 2010?

4 Before the victory in 2010, the last man to score a winning goal for Leeds at Old Trafford did so in a League encounter in February 1981. Can you name him?

5 And which centre forward from the Revie era has scored more times against the old enemy than any other Leeds player?

6 Who is the last player to have scored for Leeds against Man United in a top-flight League fixture?

7 A Norwegian right-back was the last Leeds man to be sent off in a Roses clash, receiving his marching orders in the 3–0 defeat in May 1998. Can you name him?

8 Which legendary defender has made the most League appearances in a Leeds shirt against Man United?

9 And which Leeds right-back is famously remembered as the man who could 'tame' George Best?

10 In which season was our success on winning the First Division Championship made all the sweeter when our old foes suffered relegation to the Second Division?

11 And finally, on the penultimate weekend of the 1991/92 campaign, which team did we beat and who defeated Man United to confirm us as Champions?

FACT OR FICTION?

Leeds' record home attendance was 52,368 in the First Division clash with Man United in April 1965.

Round
9

Name
that Player

Time, now, for a novelty round that has a bit of a 1980s TV quiz show feel about it. The name of the game is to identify six different players in as few clues as possible – simple, eh? And if you manage to identify a player from the first clue, the star prize is all yours: no, not a speed boat; not even a crystal decanter or his 'n' hers matching watches; you can take home a smug sense of self-satisfaction. So go on, what are you waiting for? Name that player!

Player A

1   Born in London on 1 January 1950; he began his professional footballing career at Watford.

2   England international who won 10 of his 17 senior caps during his three-season Leeds stint.

3   Arrived at Elland Road following a big-money move from Sheffield United in the summer of 1976.

4 Scored some memorable goals, including a 'banana-shot'
against Southampton that won *The Big Match* Goal of
the Season in 1978/79.

5 Flamboyant midfielder whose vision and passing ability
made him a real crowd-pleaser.

Player B

1 Touted as a future England international in his teens, although he never quite fulfilled that early potential.
2 Signed by Eddie Gray from Aston Villa for £30,000; made his Leeds debut at Oldham in February 1985.
3 Served Leeds for eight years and was a key member of the side that reached the FA Cup semi-final and play-offs in 1986/87.
4 Became the youngest FA Cup final goalkeeper in 1975, the same year in which he won the PFA Young Player of the Year award.
5 Kept 17 clean sheets during our 1989/90 promotion-winning season, before moving down the pecking order on our top-flight return.

Player C

1 Began his footballing career with St Mirren, from where Don Revie signed him for £30,000 in 1972.
2 Represented his country (Scotland) at full international level on 30 occasions.
3 Scored 3 goals during our 1974/75 European Cup campaign, but missed the final after his dismissal at Barcelona in the semis.
4 Departed Elland Road in 1978, joining Man United for a then British record transfer fee of £495,000.
5 Tall central defender who formed a formidable partnership with Hunter following Charlton's retirement.

Player D

1 Set a bizarre record in 2001, becoming the youngest player to have his boots sponsored at the tender age of 14.

2 Became the youngest player to appear in the Premier League, aged 16 years and 129 days, when he made his Leeds debut at Spurs in 2003.

3 Selected for England's 2006 World Cup finals squad at the age of 19, despite being uncapped at the time.

4 His pace and skill made this winger an Elland Road favourite during his two seasons with the club.

5 He was sold to Tottenham Hotspur for a paltry £1 million in June 2005 amid our financial meltdown.

Player E

1 Born in Melbourne, Australia, in 1965; made his professional football debut with Aston Villa.

2 Played for England in the 1990 World Cup third place play-off match against Italy and won a total of 15 senior caps.

3 Scored our second goal in the 4–3 Charity Shield victory over Liverpool in 1992.

4 Won a League Championship winners' medal and the club's Player of the Year award during his first season at Elland Road.

5 Talented left-back signed from Chelsea by Howard Wilkinson in 1991 for a fee of £1.3 million.

Player F

1 Won a Scottish FA Cup winners' medal with Aberdeen in 1970 aged just 17.
2 Was brought to Elland Road by Jimmy Armfield in the summer of 1977 for £125,000.
3 Played for Scotland on 10 occasions, with all of those caps gained during his six years with Leeds.
4 Proved to be a useful source of goals, with 3 hat-tricks among the 47 goals he scored for the club.
5 Predominantly a left-winger, he made 260 Leeds appearances before moving to Man United in 1983.

FIVES AND FOURS

Between 1990 and 1994, Howard Wilkinson signed five players directly from his former club Sheffield Wednesday. How many of them can you name?

We was Robbed

I know fans of other teams will say that plenty of refereeing decisions have gone against them over the years and that's certainly true – it's all part of the game; you win some, you lose some; swings and roundabouts and all that. It's just that some of our worst refereeing injustices occurred in vitally important games, and robbed the club of hard-earned honours. So clear your mind and try to control the bitterness as you tackle this round which, be warned, contains some of our worst travesties of justice.

1 Let's start with the big one: who scored the controversially disallowed goal in the infamous 1975 European Cup final defeat to Bayern Munich?

2 And can you name the German captain who was lucky not to have two penalties awarded against him in the first half?

3 Last one on 1975, then I'll try to move on … can you name the controversial referee?

4 Also in Europe, who were Leeds' opponents in the European Cup Winners' Cup final in 1973, during which a scandalous refereeing display saw us denied three cast-iron penalties and penalised for an innocuous-looking tackle that led to the winning goal?

5 And what was the nationality of the ultimately discredited referee?

6 Who were the Spanish opponents in a Champions League group clash at Elland Road in 2000, when the Norwegian referee, Terje Hauge, unaccountably added 4 minutes of injury time, during which period the away team equalised?

7 And a final European question for now: which Spanish team's crucial first goal in the 2001 Champions League semi-final defeat was clearly assisted into the net by the player's arm?

8 Controversial refereeing decisions against Leeds haven't just been restricted to European clashes. This next incident, occurring in the League, is indelibly scorched on most Leeds fans' memories; so, which team *was* it that scored the infamous 'offside' goal at Elland Road in April 1971?

9 And can you name the refereeing official that day who, from his perfect vantage point 20 yards behind play, overruled the linesman to wave play on?

10 Terry Cooper and Peter Lorimer each had a goal disallowed late on in our 1–0 FA Cup semi-final defeat in 1967. Which of our arch rivals got the better of the refereeing decisions that day to progress to the final?

11 In 1972, Leeds had to play the final, championship-deciding game of the season just 48 hours after appearing in the FA Cup final. The fixture ended in a 2–1 defeat, with Revie bemoaning three denied penalty shouts. But who were the opponents?

FACT OR FICTION?

Billy Bremner won the coveted Leeds United Player of the Year award on two occasions.

Round

II

It'll be all 'White' on the Night

Although we have unquestionably suffered more than our fair share of footballing travesties and refereeing howlers over the years, it's fair to say we have at times been the architects of our own sorry downfall. We may (almost) be able to smile about it now, but at the time it really was terrible! So gird your loins as you prepare to tackle this grim group of gaffes, own goals and misdemeanours.

1 Which young defender, playing in only his second League game for Leeds, scored a goal at each end in the first half of the Championship fixture against Hull City in August 2011?

2 Who scored a notorious own goal at a snow-covered Anfield in December 1967?

3   Can you name the Leeds captain who delayed the
    promotion party in May 2010 by scoring a late own goal
    in the 1–0 defeat at Charlton?

4   And in the final emotionally fraught match of that
    season, we beat Bristol Rovers 2–1 at Elland Road to
    win promotion back to the Championship despite being
    down to ten men. Can you recall the name of the irate
    winger who refused to leave the field of play after being
    shown a red card in the first half of that match?

5   Also on the theme of red cards, which Leeds player was
    sent off for retaliation 2 minutes before the end of the
    infamous 1973 European Cup Winners' Cup final against
    AC Milan?

6   Our seven-match winning streak at the start of the
    2007/08 season was eventually halted by Gillingham in
    a game that we finished with only nine players. Can you
    name our two strikers who were both sent off after
    receiving two yellow cards?

7   We also finished the 2005/06 League One play-off
    semi-final second leg against Preston with just nine
    players. Stephen Crainey was sent off midway through
    the second half, but can you recall the striker who
    came on with just 11 minutes to go and still managed to
    receive a red card after two bookings?

8　And which two Leeds players received red cards in the 2–1 home defeat at the hands of Brighton in April 2013?

9　A First Division clash on 7 November 1964 became so violent and ill-tempered that referee Ken Stokes took the players from the pitch for 10 minutes before half-time in an attempt to cool things down. Who were our opponents in that infamous game?

10　And in February 1966 a game at Elland Road boiled over and players were taken from the pitch for a cooling-off period with 15 minutes of the game remaining. Who were our cynical Spanish opponents in that Inter-Cities Fairs Cup clash?

11　Finally, in November 2011 a disastrous first half against Blackpool at Elland Road saw us concede 3 goals. Can you name the hapless goalkeeper who had a nightmare between the sticks and was substituted at half-time?

FACT OR FICTION?

During our 1989/90 promotion-winning season, 'Psycho' Vinnie Jones was only sent off once.

The Last is
the First

Time now for a round with a bit of a twist. The answers to the eleven questions are all surnames of Leeds United players past or present. However, to help you along your way, the last letter of the first player's surname is also the first letter of the next, and so on – so the answers form a kind of chain. Just get the first question right and the rest should be a breeze!

1 Right-back who joined Leeds from relegated Charlton in 1999. He made his England international debut while at Elland Road and went on to play in the 2002 World Cup finals.

2 Legendary Welsh midfielder who emerged from the club's youth ranks to make his first-team debut in 1989. Made over 300 appearances for Leeds United before departing for Everton in 1996.

3 Controversial, much-maligned Senegalese forward who arrived at Elland Road in August 2012. Rose from 'sewer rat' to 'matador' in Neil Warnock's opinion!

4 Central defender who joined Leeds from Tottenham Hotspur in 1989 and made his debut on the same day as Gordon Strachan. Was voted Supporters' Player of the Year in his first full season at Elland Road.

5 Recipient of the first ever PFA Players' Player of the Year award in 1973/74, this legendary defender was fiercely competitive in the challenge.

6 Veteran Welsh striker who spent the 1996/97 season at Elland Road when in the twilight of his illustrious footballing career. Fair to say he wasn't a runaway success at Leeds, though, scoring only three times in 36 League outings.

7 Northern Ireland striker who joined Leeds in October 2004 and finished the season as joint top scorer, a feat he equalled the following season and exceeded in 2006/07 when he topped the goalscoring charts on his own. He scored the only goal in his country's famous victory over England in a 2005 World Cup qualifier.

8   Combative Welsh midfielder who joined the club as an apprentice in 1967 but initially struggled to command a regular place in Revie's starting XI. Eventually amassed almost 200 appearances in 10 seasons, including several prestigious finals, before being sent to Coventry.

9   Norwegian defender who played for Leeds between 1997 and 2000; famously had a long-standing feud with Man United's Roy Keane.

10   Signed from Blackburn in 2005, this Republic of Ireland midfielder impressively picked up 15 yellow cards in 37 appearances during our 2006/07 nightmare season. He left Elland Road in 2009 and joined Swindon Town.

11   Talented midfielder possessing vision and skill in abundance, this player made his Leeds debut in 1982 and was rarely out of the team for the next seven years. He fell out of favour when Wilkinson took over the managerial reins and left for Nottingham Forest, where he played only one game before joining Sheffield Wednesday.

FIVES AND FOURS

Leeds United provided five players for the 1974 Scotland World Cup finals squad. Can you name them?

Leeds!
Leeds!
Leeds!

The grand city of Leeds has produced many famous sons and daughters. Political leaders, authors, artists and musicians rank amongst the city's most illustrious children. The maternity units of local hospitals have also spawned many successful sportsmen, including a fair old smattering of talented footballers. Countless youngsters from the Leeds area may have dreamt of pulling on one of those famous white shirts, but only an elite group of Loiners have actually managed to turn that dream into reality. So enjoy this round which tests your knowledge of the local boys who succeeded in playing for their hometown club – the pride of Leeds!

1 Left-sided home-grown talent who made his first-team debut in August 2008 at the age of 16; his early playing career was blighted by bouts of cramp towards the end of games.

2   Winger signed in 2010 from Charlton Athletic, whose
    Leeds career began badly when he conceded a penalty
    on his debut against Derby County; he left the club and
    country in 2012, to join the New York Red Bulls.

3   Tenacious midfielder who made a total of 301 League
    appearances for Leeds and scored just 4 goals, despite
    being encouraged to 'Shoot!' whenever he got the ball
    in the opposition's half.

4   Leeds United's most versatile player ever, this class act
    played in every position except goal during his incredible
    17-year Elland Road career.

5   Massive Leeds United fan who scored in the first leg of
    the 1993 FA Youth Cup final at Old Trafford; this striker
    went on to make 48 first-team League appearances
    before reluctantly leaving West Yorkshire to join
    Coventry City in 1995.

6   Hometown hero-turned-villain who won the Leeds United
    Player of the Year award two years running in 2002/03 and
    2003/04 – a first in the club's history.

7   Another recipient of the Player of the Year award, this
    time in 1994/95. Returned to his hometown club for a
    second spell in 2004 and famously scored 4 goals in a
    6–1 victory over QPR.

8   Rated the best goalkeeper in the 1974 World Cup, this Leeds-born goalie signed by Revie in 1965 left to join Vancouver Whitecaps but couldn't resist a return to his hometown in the '80s.

9   Midfielder who emerged from the Leeds youth ranks to play for the team he supported as a boy. Reluctantly left Elland Road in 2004 to join Newcastle United.

10 Classy winger of Irish descent who played for Leeds between 1965 and 1969. Scored the club's first-ever goal in the European Cup when he netted after 35 seconds in the 10–0 drubbing of Lyn Oslo in 1969.

11 Blond-haired striker who scored on his 20th birthday in 1981, prompting a spontaneous rendition of 'Happy Birthday' from the Elland Road faithful; left Leeds just two years later to further his education.

FACT OR FICTION?

The club's greatest right back, Paul Reaney, was born in Leeds.

Round

14

Hot Shots

When my son comes home from playing football, the second question I always ask – after ascertaining the result – is who scored the goals. And so it is with any football game at whatever level. Goalscorers are the glory boys, the ones who soak up all the praise and adulation, the ones most adored by the fans. And we've certainly had a few players down the years who've known how to find the back of the net on a regular basis. So go on, give this round of questions your best shot, and see how many you can score!

1   Which Leeds legend holds the club record for scoring the most League goals?

2   And who holds the record, set in 1953/54, for scoring the most League goals in a season?

3   A toughie now: which prolific Leeds striker scored a hat-trick in three consecutive First Division matches in 1926/27?

4   In February 1972, who scored a hat-trick against old foes Man United, and remains to date the only Leeds player to have achieved this feat in the post-war period?

5   And which player scored a 'perfect' 15-minute hat-trick away at Scunthorpe in October 2010, scoring with his left foot, his right foot and his head?

6   A final one on hat-tricks: in April 1991, who scored three times against Liverpool at Elland Road but still ended up on the losing side?

7   Can you recall the player who scored all 4 Leeds goals in a memorable 4–3 victory over Liverpool at Elland Road in November 2000?

8   And who also scored all 4 goals in a match at Elland Road, this time in a 4–0 victory over Burnley in 1971?

9   In 2008/09, who became the first Leeds player in over thirty years to score 30 goals in a season?

10 Which hotshot remains the only Leeds United player to win successive BBC *Match of the Day* Goal of the Month competitions, a feat achieved in September and October 1995?

11   And finally, which Leeds United striker was joint winner
     of the Premier League Golden Boot award in 1998/99?

FACT OR FICTION?

*Luciano Becchio ended the 2012/13 season as
Leeds United's top goalscorer.*

Super Stoppers

While strikers are the undisputed glory boys, goalkeepers must surely have the most thankless of jobs in a football team. They can perform magnificently for 89 minutes, but find themselves berated at the end of the game for a solitary lapse of concentration – and it is these occasional mistakes that tend to live longest in our unforgiving memories. Makes you wonder why anyone would want to be a goalkeeper! Luckily for us, though, we have had a surfeit of candidates hoping to fill the Number One position at Elland Road over the years and I feel they deserve to be honoured in this quiz book. So here we go with a round devoted to those strange footballers who are allowed to use their hands – where would we be without them?

1 Which goalkeeper, who made his first-team debut for
Leeds in 1979, spent his entire career at just two clubs; he
had two spells at each and won the League title with both?

2 In March 1962, a teenager was flown from Leeds to
Southampton to make an unexpected first-team debut
when the regular keeper fell ill on the morning of the
game. Can you name the young stopper who went on to
make over 500 appearances for Leeds?

3 A dramatic League Cup tie against Swindon in 2003
produced a memorable night for our keeper: he scored
a goal in the dying seconds to take the tie to extra time
and then saved a penalty in the shoot-out to clinch
victory. Who was our heroic custodian that night?

4 Can you name the Danish goalkeeper who was
outstanding in keeping a clean sheet against Man United
in our famous 2010 FA Cup victory?

5 And, in his only season at Elland Road, which other
Dane was voted Player of the 2010/11 FA Cup
Third Round, following a series of superb saves in the tie
against Arsenal?

6 Which fans' favourite – whose transfer from Crystal
Palace to Leeds in 1996 made him Britain's most expensive
goalkeeper – is the oldest Leeds player to play for England?

7   And which Scottish international, signed from Chelsea by Kevin Blackwell in the summer of 2004, was voted the club's Player of the Year in his first season at Elland Road?

8   Which keeper was reunited with manager Neil Warnock for a fourth time in his career when he joined Leeds in July 2012?

9   In 1982, manager Eddie Gray allowed a young apprentice to leave the club and join Peterborough for £4,000. That young keeper went on to make a bit of a name for himself elsewhere. Can you name the Rotherham-born custodian who slipped through our fingers?

10 In 1975, David Harvey was injured in a car accident and missed the European Cup final against Bayern Munich, but can you name the goalkeeper who deputised for him in the Paris showdown?

11 And finally, in the 1995/96 season, which central defender deputised in goal against both Middlesbrough and Man United when the regular keepers were injured and sent off respectively?

FIVES AND FOURS

Name the five players to have appeared in goal for Leeds United on the most occasions.

Three Lions
on a Shirt

Supply may have dried up somewhat in more recent years, but over the decades Leeds United has proved to be a rich source of English talent, contributing many outstanding footballers to the England cause. But how much do you know about the Englishmen from Leeds United who have had the honour of representing their country?

1 The last Leeds player to score a goal for the full England team did so in a friendly against Portugal in 2002. Can you name the player?

2 Willis Edwards was the first Leeds United player to captain England; only one other Leeds player has skippered the senior England team, doing so in 1980. Can you name him?

3 Jack Charlton was famously a key member of England's 1966 World Cup-winning team. But which other Leeds player was in the 1966 World Cup-winning squad, although he didn't appear in any of the games?

4 And which future Leeds manager was also included in the victorious World Cup squad, although he too failed to feature in any of the games?

5 Can you name the Leeds striker who made his international debut at the 1970 World Cup finals?

6 Which Leeds defender played every single minute for England in the same campaign?

7 And which unfortunate Leeds defensive man missed out on a place in the 1970 World Cup squad after breaking his leg in a League fixture at West Ham in April 1970?

8 Leeds United provided one player for England's 1998 World Cup finals squad. Who was it?

9 In 1977, which Leeds defender became the first and remains, to date, the only player to be sent off for England whilst playing in a friendly?

10 Three former Leeds managers have also taken charge of the full England team. Can you name them?

11 And finally, three former Leeds United players suffered the ignominy of being included in BBC Three's worst-ever England football team: can you name this unfortunate trio?

FACT OR FICTION?

Elland Road was a host ground for Euro 96, but has never staged a full England international match.

What's in a Name?

And now, as Monty Python would say, for something completely different! For each of the questions in this round I've given the nickname of a Leeds United player and also a clue to his identity. All you have to do is correctly identify the eleven players. If you manage to name a player without the clue, award yourself a big gold star!

1 **Lash**: A true Leeds legend who made his debut in 1962, this player's powerful shooting earned him his nickname.

2 **Zico**: Popular defender who signed from Glasgow Rangers in 1989, and possessed a pretty decent shot himself!

3 **The Black Flash**: Fondly remembered by Leeds fans of the 1960s, this silky winger illuminated games with his sublime skills.

4 **Jasper**: The most expensive full-back in the land when signed from Blackburn in 1979, this player suffered relegation with Leeds and left to join Burnley in 1984.

5 **The Gentle Giant**: Often referred to as the most complete player ever to don a Leeds shirt, the West Stand's name was changed in tribute to this Welsh genius following his death in 2004.

6 **Jaws**: Powerful striker from the 1970s who terrified opposing defences, this Scottish international left Leeds to join old foes Man United in 1978.

7 **Big Bird**: Beanpole striker who joined Leeds from Charlton in 1987. His finest hour came when he scored a hat-trick against Sheffield United in 1988.

8 **The Terminator**: Bulky Dutch defender signed by George Graham in 1997. Injury curtailed his Leeds career and he departed to join neighbours Bradford City in 2000.

9 **Smudge**: Local boy who rose through the Leeds youth ranks and scored with his first touch of the ball in his first-team debut against Liverpool in 1998.

10 **Giraffe**: Imperious centre half who made his debut for Leeds in 1953 and went on to make over 700 appearances for the club.

II **The Chief**: Highly esteemed former captain who made 200 League appearances for Leeds between 1994 and 2005 – but surely his greatest honour was having the Kop Cat named after him!

FIVES AND FOURS

Four players whose surnames begin with 'M' have been voted outright winners of the Leeds United Player of the Year award: one of those recipients won the coveted award in 1975 and 1977, the other three in 1976, 1994 and 1997. Can you name all four players?

We've had our Ups and Downs...

I think it's fair to say that being a Leeds United fan has never been a particularly easy occupation. Although we have enjoyed long spells of security in the top flight of English football, we have, at other times, found ourselves fighting desperate relegation battles and on more than one occasion have had to endure the sickening sensation of plunging headlong over the edge of the precipice. Prepare to relive the agony and the ecstasy with this rollercoaster round all about relegation heartbreak and promotion-winning success.

I In the early years, Leeds United was regarded as a bit of a yo-yo club. How many times in its first twelve years was the club relegated then promoted straight back to the top flight the following season?

2 Don Revie's first full season in charge almost ended catastrophically in relegation to the Third Division. From which north-east team did we need to take a point on the final day of the 1961/62 season to guarantee our Second Division survival?

3 Revie's team won promotion to the First Division in the 1963/64 campaign, ushering in the glory days at Elland Road. Who was the inspirational captain who led us to promotion and the title that season?

4 The last echoes of the glory days were silenced once and for all in May 1982, when we suffered the pain of relegation to the Second Division. At which ground was our fate sealed, amidst distinctly inglorious scenes of crowd trouble?

5 In 1986/87 we almost escaped football's second tier when we reached the play-off final – but fell agonisingly short at the final hurdle. Against which team did we play 3 games in that final, eventually succumbing to two late extra-time goals in the third game?

6 Promotion from the second tier was eventually achieved three seasons later. But victory over which South Coast club in May 1990 ultimately secured our return to the top flight?

7   And in which season did 'living the dream' turn into a
    nightmare as we relinquished our Premier League status?

8   In the 2005/06 season we almost bounced back
    to the Premier League with an appearance in the
    Championship play-off final against Watford. Can you
    name the manager who guided us to the Millennium
    Stadium finale?

9   With Leeds United's fortunes in terminal decline, who
    were the opponents at Elland Road on 28 April 2007, on
    a black day that saw us all but relegated to the third tier
    of English football for the first time in the club's history?

10 We almost made a return to the Championship at the first time of asking when we reached the play-off final against Doncaster Rovers in May 2008. What was the score in that Wembley showdown?

11 We did finally secure our return to the Championship after a tense final-day 2–1 victory over Bristol Rovers at Elland Road in May 2010. Jonny Howson came off the bench to score our equaliser but who was the stand-in skipper who played a captain's role by grabbing the winner?

FACT OR FICTION?

Leeds United have spent more seasons in the second tier of English football than in the top flight.

The 'Other' Cup

First contested in the 1960/61 season, the Football League Cup was the brainchild of former secretary of the Football League, Alan Hardaker. Although it has never really inspired the kind of passion that is felt for the FA Cup, the League Cup, in its many guises, has nevertheless afforded Leeds some glorious memories, a couple of Wembley outings and, most importantly, it has provided a nice, shiny addition to the trophy cabinet. So take your chances and see how far you can progress in this Leeds United League Cup challenge.

1   During Don Revie's tenure as manager, how many times did Leeds progress beyond the fourth round of the League Cup?

2   Who were our opponents in the 1968 Final, which ended in a 1–0 victory for Leeds?

3   And can you name the imperious left back who dreamt about scoring the winner in the final and then did?

4 Leeds have reached the League Cup final on one other occasion, in 1996. Can you recall our Wembley opponents that year?

5 The 1996 League Cup final may have ended in bitter disappointment, but can you remember the Midlands club that we overcame in the semi-final to book our place at Wembley?

6 And which Leeds striker scored in both legs of the semi-final, including a memorable scissor-kick in the second leg at Elland Road?

7   In 1990/91, our first season back in the top flight, we tasted defeat in the semi-final of the League Cup. But can you recall the opponents that ended our Wembley dreams that year?

8   One of the League Cup's biggest ever shocks occurred in 1974/75, when we were ousted from the competition at the fourth round stage. Which Fourth Division side inflicted a 3–0 defeat to send us crashing out of that season's competition?

9   In the 2012/13 season, we went on a bit of a 'giant-killing' spree ourselves. Can you remember which two Premier League teams we knocked out of the League Cup during that campaign?

10 And which top-flight team finally defeated us at the quarter-final stage?

11 Returning right back to the beginning, in October 1960 who became the first Leeds United player to score a goal in the League Cup?

FIVES AND FOURS

Name the four players who have scored the most goals for Leeds in the League Cup.

White Hot Debuts

We've all been there; one of the crowd waiting in eager anticipation to witness the debut of an exciting young prospect or new club signing. All players must desperately hope to make a winning start, to put in a 'man of the match' performance and become an instant fans' favourite. And, although many must dream about kicking off their time at a new club with a priceless debut-day goal, only a select few actually manage to turn that dream into reality. The players in this round all belong to that elite group of Leeds United goalscoring debutants. See how many of them you can remember.

I   Two players both scored on their Leeds United debuts during the 4–0 League Cup victory over Shrewsbury Town in August 2012. Can you name either of our goalscoring debutants?

2   Which forward, who topped the club's League scoring charts in the 2005/06 season, made a dream debut when scoring 2 spectacular long-range goals during a 3–1 victory over Reading in February 2005?

3   A Welsh international – who became the most expensive Third Division player when he moved from Swansea to Leeds in 1979 – also grabbed 2 debut-day goals. But can you name the striker who soon returned to the valleys after struggling to make an impression at Elland Road?

4   And which Welsh international winger, signed by Don Revie, made a memorable start in his first League game when he came off the bench to grab the winning goal in a 2–1 victory over Ipswich Town in April 1975 aged just 18?

5   Another teenage prodigy who made a goalscoring debut netted against Fulham in April 1983. Can you name the young Scot that we subsequently sold to Oldham when aged just 20, even though he topped our goalscoring charts in his first two seasons with the club?

6   And which other popular striker that we also sold to Oldham Athletic scored on his Leeds debut against Crystal Palace in March 1983?

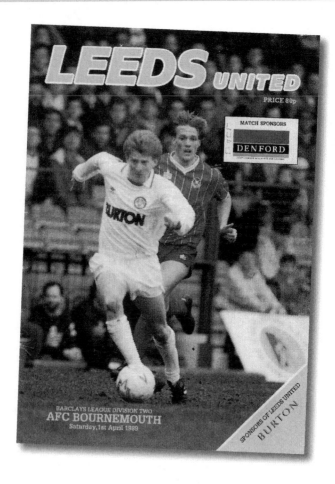

7 Which striker, signed from Bristol City by Howard Wilkinson, made an instant Elland Road impact with a debut-day hat-trick against Bournemouth in April 1989?

8   Another Wilkinson signing also scored on his Leeds debut, this time against Middlesbrough in January 1993. But can you name the homesick Norwegian striker who added just one more goal to his tally during his brief and unsuccessful Elland Road stint?

9   Easier one now: which Dutch international striker, signed by George Graham in 1997, scored on his debut and then finished as the club's leading goalscorer in both of the seasons that he graced the Elland Road turf?

10 Which striker scored on his debut against Swindon Town in 1987 following his transfer from Derby County and went on to become a cult hero during our promotion push in 1989/90?

11 Finally, a player signed from Glasgow Rangers also scored on his Leeds debut in March 1980. Can you name the Scottish international striker who then added just 9 more goals in his next 52 Leeds appearances before moving to Man City?

FACT OR FICTION?

Albert Johanneson was Leeds United's first black player.

Connect
Four

Time now for a bit of a pub quiz favourite. All you have to do is identify the names of four players from the clues provided and then work out what they all have in common. There are four sets of players and four connections for you to have a go at. I've meticulously researched this round and I am confident that there is only one sensible Leeds-related connection between each set of players, but if you do dredge up another you can award yourself a point. Oh, and it's never just 'they all played for Leeds' – that goes without saying!

Connect 1

1 Inspirational captain and ferocious tackler who dropped down a division to join Leeds in 1962; proved to be the catalyst for the team's remarkable success during the Revie era.

2 Another influential skipper who also elected to transfer to a lower division in 1989 and in the process rejuvenated both his own career and the team's fortunes.

3 Continuing the captain's theme: the most successful skipper in our club's history – need I say more!

4 Centre half who spent his whole career at Elland Road; ended his 21-year illustrious association with the club in 1973 after making more Leeds appearances than any other player.

So, what's the connection between this gang of four?

Connect 2

1 Legendary Leeds striker who had to be helped up the Wembley steps to collect his FA Cup winners' medal in 1972 after dislocating his elbow in the dying embers of the game.

2 England international winger who moved to West Yorkshire in 1981 with a big reputation derived mainly from his early days with Man City; did nothing to enhance that reputation at Elland Road, though, simply proving to be the wrong player at the wrong time for Leeds.

3 Exciting young prospect who joined Leeds in 1999 from Sunderland and showed great promise in his first season, but a succession of injuries over the next four years ensured that this striker never fulfilled that potential.

4 Central defender who spent two seasons at Elland Road, the second as club captain. He departed in the summer of 2002 amid the club's growing financial turmoil after an impressive World Cup finals tournament with England.

And what connects these four players?

Connect 3

1   Fiercely competitive midfielder who was brave
    enough to take one of England's penalties in the 1998
    World Cup shoot-out against Argentina although,
    despite us all willing him on, the end result was perhaps
    somewhat inevitable.

2   Rotherham-born striker whose wholehearted displays
    and aggressive spirit earned him a booking or two but also
    made him a firm fans' favourite. He twice topped the Leeds
    scoring charts (in 1985/86 and 1986/87) and was also
    voted the Supporters' Player of the Year (in 1988/89).

3   Frail-looking midfielder who made his Leeds debut
    in May 1983 when aged just 17. He went on to prove
    that artistry and skill can sometimes overcome a lack
    of physical prowess. Sadly for us, his best days were
    arguably with Blackburn, not at Elland Road.

4   Scottish left-sided full-back or midfielder from a
    footballing dynasty who played almost 400 games for
    Leeds in the 1970s and '80s; became the first player
    to appear in a European Cup final with two different
    English clubs after becoming reacquainted with Brian
    Clough at Nottingham Forest.

    And what's this group of four got in common?

Connect 4

1   Scottish international winger signed from Livingston in 2008; a crowd favourite who won both the Players' and Supporters' Player of the Year awards in 2011/12.

2   Home-grown midfielder who made his club debut in 2006. He first captained the side at the tender age of 19 when he led the team out for a League One fixture at Millwall in April 2008.

3   This midfield player moved to Leeds from Northampton in 2008. He became a regular under Simon Grayson before a protracted and somewhat acrimonious Elland Road departure in 2011.

4   Popular Argentinian striker who joined Leeds in 2008 after five seasons with lower league Spanish clubs; scored 76 League goals during his five seasons in West Yorkshire.

And finally, what's the connection between these four former Leeds players?

FIVES AND FOURS

Four Leeds players were included in the PFA Premier League Team of the Year in 2000. Can you name them?

Round 22

Sergeant Wilko's Barmy Army

Time now for a stroll down memory lane to another successful era in our club's long and distinguished history. When Howard Wilkinson arrived at Elland Road we were settling into our seventh consecutive season of Second Division football; within an incredibly short space of time he had transformed the team into First Division Champions! So enjoy this round that looks back on our rapid rise to success and see what you can remember about the time we all served in Sergeant Wilko's barmy army!

1   Wilkinson took over the managerial reins at Elland Road in October 1988, but which popular manager did he succeed?

2 Throughout our entire promotion-winning season of 1989/90 our home form was imperious, with only one team claiming a League victory over us at Elland Road. But can you recall the visitors who snatched all three points in our penultimate home game of the season?

3 As the 1989/90 campaign came to a climax, three 'Uniteds' were all still in with a chance of clinching the title and promotion on the final day. Can you remember which United ultimately finished runners-up and which just missed out on promotion that season?

4 And which striker, who left Leeds for Middlesbrough in January 1990, did us a favour on the final day of the season when scoring twice for his new club to seal victory over one of our promotion challengers?

5 A final question on our promotion-winning season: which inspirational player found the back of the net more times than anyone else for Leeds to finish as leading goalscorer that season?

6 Our first game back in the top tier of English football was an away fixture across the Pennines. We made a winning start to our campaign with a 3–2 victory, but can you recall the team that we defeated in that opening top-flight clash?

7   Which fans' favourite and long-throw specialist departed Elland Road for Sheffield United in September 1990 after featuring in just one top-flight game for Leeds?

8   Also on the theme of transfers, Wilkinson signed our first two £1 million players in the summer of 1990. Both went on to feature in every League game in 1990/91 and our Championship-winning campaign the following season. Can you name the two dependable ever-present players?

9   During our outstanding 1991/92 campaign, can you remember how many times we suffered defeat in the League at Elland Road?

10 In January 1992 we experienced one of our more enjoyable away games, running out as 6–1 victors in a somewhat one-sided affair. Can you recall the opposition that day who actually ended the season third in the table?

11 And which prolific striker, who scored a hat-trick in that game, finished our glorious Championship-winning season as the club's leading goalscorer?

FACT OR FICTION?

> *Howard Wilkinson is the last English manager to win the top-flight League title in England.*

The Price
is 'White'

All the fun of the transfer market merry-go-round now!
Of course, some of our very best, most influential players have
been home-grown starlets, rising meteorically through the youth
ranks and maturing over time into Leeds legends. However, over
the years, the transfer market has inevitably provided a wealth
of talented – and perhaps a few not-so-talented – players who
have been lured away from other clubs to join the Leeds ranks.
It works the other way too, of course, and, just occasionally, our
hearts have been broken as we've waved goodbye.

1   Let's kick off with a relatively easy one: who became
    the world's most expensive defender when he joined
    us from West Ham in November 2000?

2   And which midfielder became the most expensive
    British teenager when we signed him from Charlton
    Athletic in 1996?

3 One of our best-ever signings arrived at Elland Road from Man United in August 1963. Can you name the influential midfielder that Don Revie signed for £33,000 from our arch rivals?

4 Howard Wilkinson more than returned that favour when he allowed which influential player to cross the Pennines and move to Old Trafford for a derisory fee in November 1992?

5 In 1993, Wilkinson also sanctioned an exchange deal with Manchester's other club involving two 'Davids'. But can you remember the David that we signed from Man City and the David that left Leeds for Maine Road?

6 Andy Ritchie moved to Elland Road from Brighton in 1983 in another exchange deal. But which Leeds-born striker, who had made a goalscoring senior club debut at the age of 17 just four years earlier, was the player who moved to the South Coast club?

7 Which two players were signed by Brian Clough from Derby County in August 1974 and then followed him to Nottingham Forest after enduring a torrid six months at Elland Road?

8 Clough also brought a sublimely talented forward to Elland Road for a then club-record fee. Can you recall the name of this popular player who went on to top Leeds' scoring charts in 1975/76?

9 Ross McCormack also topped the club's goalscoring charts during his second season at Elland Road. But from which club did we sign the Scottish international striker in August 2010?

10 And from which Premier League club did we sign Stephen Warnock in the January 2013 transfer window?

11 Finally, it's fair to say that Seth Johnson was not our shrewdest ever acquisition. But to which club did we hand over £7 million in 2001 to secure the services of the England international midfielder?

FIVES AND FOURS

Which four players moved from Portsmouth to Elland Road in the summer of 2012?

The Life and Times of Leeds United

Over the years, Elland Road has been populated with an array of talented individuals and colourful characters. And we, the supporters, have obsessively followed the trials and tribulations, hard-fought battles and hard-earned victories surrounding those individuals both on and off the pitch. It's fortunate for us, therefore, that some of Elland Road's main protagonists have chosen to write about their experiences in football. This round features fifteen of those biographical works: all you have to do is name the player the book is about! But don't worry, I'm throwing you a lifeline: if you're struggling, all the players are listed at the bottom of page 86 – just find the correct pairings!

1 *Sniffer*
2 *In My Defence*
3 *The Last Fancy Dan*
4 *Leeds United's Rolls Royce*
5 *Soccer's Happy Wanderer*
6 *Boozing, Betting and Brawling*
7 *Behind the Dream: The Story of a Scottish Footballer*
8 *Careless Hands*
9 *One Hump or Two?*
10 *Hard Man, Hard Knocks*
11 *Mr Unbelievable*
12 *Biting Talk*
13 *Leeds United on Trial*
14 *King John*
15 *My Life in Football*

John Charles, Allan Clarke, Norman Hunter, Joe Jordan,
Chris Kamara, Paul Madeley, Dominic Matteo, Duncan McKenzie,
David O'Leary, Don Revie, Gordon Strachan, Gary Sprake,
Mel Sterland, Frank Worthington, Terry Yorath

FACT OR FICTION?

**Snod This for a Laugh *is the autobiography
of former Leeds winger Robert Snodgrass.***

We are the Champions, Champions of Europe!

Leeds United has a long and illustrious history in European competitions and on many occasions we have tasted heady success in sultry foreign climes. Although it may be some time since we last locked competitive horns with our continental neighbours, the memories still burn bright and it's worth reflecting on the contribution we have made to European football through the decades. So dust off your passports as we prepare to take a whistle-stop tour to relive our great European adventures!

1   OK, let's start back at the very beginning. In which competition did we play our first-ever European fixture?

2   And do you know which influential midfielder scored our first goal in European football?

3 Our 1973 Cup Winners' Cup final appearance is infamous, but can you recall our Yugoslav semi-final opponents in that campaign, who we defeated with a 1–0 victory at Elland Road which we then defended in the away leg?

4 The club's first ever venture in the European Cup was in 1969/70. The first-round first-leg game of that campaign resulted in a 10–0 win, which remains our record victory in Europe. Who were our opponents?

5 Our first Champions League campaign in 1992/93 saw us reach the second round in strange circumstances. Can you recall what happened in the first-round tie against VfB Stuttgart and how it was eventually decided?

6 And do you remember the super-sub striker who scored the goal that eventually saw us progress through to the second round that year?

7 A striker who spent years on the periphery of Revie's great team had his finest hour in Europe when he scored a hat-trick against Kilmarnock to secure our passage to the 1966/67 Inter-Cities Fairs Cup final. Can you name that player?

8 And which striker went one better in November 2002, scoring 4 goals in the UEFA Cup second-round second leg against Hapoel Tel Aviv?

9 Who is our all-time leading goalscorer in Europe?

10 And which legendary defender from the Revie era has made the most European appearances for the club?

11 Finally, who were our last opponents in European football who we played in a third round UEFA Cup tie in December 2002?

FIVES AND FOURS

Our last appearance in the UEFA Champions League was in 2000/01. Amongst our opponents in that campaign were four Spanish clubs. Can you name them all?

'Managing to Succeed'

This round is all about the men who have managed Leeds United. Amongst this eclectic group there are a fair few former Leeds players, along with some who made their names playing for other clubs and some who never really made it as a player at all. There are those who couldn't resist a return to Elland Road for a second managerial stint; those who moved on from Leeds to become international managers, and those who left to form more successful associations with other clubs. We have had hugely talented managers, legendary managers and, it has to be said, one or two downright disasters. So, doff your caps as we pay homage to the managers.

1   Who was in charge of Leeds United's first-ever Football League game?

2 And can you name the legendary 'military man' who guided us to the FA Cup quarter-finals in 1950 for the first time in our history?

3 Two former Leeds United players have managed the club on a permanent basis and then returned several years later for a stint as caretaker manager. Willis Edwards (1947–48 and caretaker in 1958) is one; can you name the other?

4 In 2008, which former Elland Road captain became the first man to have both skippered Leeds United at Wembley and then led the Leeds side out as manager in a competitive game at the National Stadium?

5 Under which manager did we suffer relegation to the third tier for the first time in the club's history?

6 And who was in charge of team affairs when we regained our Championship spot three years later?

7 Brian Clough was infamously Leeds manager for just forty-four days. How many games did he win during his uneasy tenure?

8 And which other manager was at the Elland Road helm for just forty-four days?

9 Two ex-Leeds players have managed the Republic of Ireland. Who are they?

10 And can you name the two former Leeds players who have managed Wales on a permanent basis?

11 Finally, from which Leeds manager's autobiography did I steal the title for this round?

FACT OR FICTION?

Prior to 2014, Leeds had never had a permanent manager born outside the British Isles.

Who Scored the Goal?

Time for a slightly different round now. Listed below are 11 Leeds United games, with details of our opponents, the venue, date, competition and final score. All you have to do is identify the player who scored the celebrated Leeds goal in each of the 11 games. Some of the goals won official recognition, some have gone down in Leeds folklore, and one is just my personal favourite that I saw scored at Elland Road. Oh, and if you need a clue I've even provided the number of letters in each scorer's name along with a couple of those letters. So go on, see how many you can remember!

I	Tottenham Hotspur	Elland Road	17 April 1994	Premier League	2–0
		_ _ D	W_ _ _ _ _ _		
2	Burnley	Elland Road	4 April 1970	First Division	2–1
		_ D_ _ _	_ _ _ Y		

3	Oldham Athletic	Boundary Park	17 May 1987	Second Division Play-offs	2—1
	K_ _ _ _		E_ _ _ _ _ _		
4	Arsenal	Elland Road	19 January 2011	FA Cup	1—3
	_ _ _ _ _ _ Y		_ _ _ _ _ _ N		
5	Leicester City	Elland Road	28 April 1990	Second Division	2—1
	_ _ _ _ _ N		S_ _ _ _ _ _ _		
6	Liverpool	Elland Road	21 August 1995	Premier League	1—0
	_ _ _ Y		_E_ _ _ _		
7	Tottenham Hotspur	Elland Road	27 January 2013	FA Cup	2—1
	R _ _ _		_ _ _ _ _ _ _ K		
8	Manchester City	Elland Road	7 September 1991	First Division	3—0
	D_ _ _ _		_ _ _ _ Y		
9	AC Milan	San Siro	8 November 2000	Champions League	1—1
	D_ _ _ _ _ _		_A_ _ _ _		
10	Manchester United	Elland Road	6 September 1969	First Division	2—2
	_ I _ _ _		_ _ _ _ E _		
11	Hull City	Elland Road	10 February 1990	Second Division	4—3
	V_ _ _ _ _		_ _ _ _ S		

FIVES AND FOURS

Between 1977/78 and 1980/81, the four players who topped the Leeds scoring charts all had surnames beginning with 'H'. How many of them can you remember?

The Kids are all 'White'

It's probably fair to say that there have been two golden eras for Leeds United's youth policy. In the 1960s and then again in the '90s a clutch of exciting, supremely talented players emerged from the youth squads to make a sensational impact on the English footballing landscape. Over the years, Leeds have not been afraid to blood youngsters in the first team and have nurtured some prodigious talent. So let's find out how much you know about the teenagers who have played for Leeds.

1 We'll start the round with the obvious question: which Leeds legend, who made his debut in September 1962, is the club's youngest-ever player?

2 And which teenager became the Premier League's youngest goalscorer on Boxing Day 2002 when he bagged a goal in the 2–1 victory at Sunderland?

3   In 1999, which defender became the only Leeds player to win a full England cap while still a teenager?

4   And can you name the Leeds player who became Wales' youngest goalkeeper when he made his full international debut in 1963 against Scotland?

5   Which talented Antipodean, named PFA Young Player of the Year in 1999/00, remains the only player to receive this award whilst at Leeds?

6   Can you name the midfielder who scooped the Football League Young Player of the Year award in 2008/09 before departing for Villa Park?

7   And a final question on awards: which youngster scooped the 'Jewson lot' at the Leeds United 2012/13 awards ceremony, winning Supporters' Player of the Year, Players' Player of the Year and Young Player of the Year?

8   The Club's youngsters won the FA Youth Cup in 1993, but can you recall which star-studded team we beat in the final?

9   And which young striker scored in both legs of the 1993 final to secure a 4–1 aggregate win?

10 In 1997, Leeds' youngsters won a second FA Youth Cup, beating Crystal Palace in the final. Can you name our goalkeeper, who went on to enjoy success with both Leeds and England?

11 Finally, which product of the Leeds United youth academy never made a first-team appearance for the club but was sold for around £1 million to Tottenham Hotspur in the summer of 2007?

FACT OR FICTION?

Before finding fame and fortune with boy band Westlife, Nicky Byrne spent two years as a goalkeeper in the Leeds youth squad.

Sweet Charity

Although our involvement in the Charity Shield may not have been extensive, it has certainly been eventful! The traditional curtain-raiser to the English football season was first contested in 1908, and since 1930 it has predominantly pitted the FA Cup winners against the English League Champions. Although we actually declined the invitation to participate following our FA Cup victory in 1972, we have been involved in several rather feisty, incident-packed encounters that have featured one or two less-than-charitable moments, as well as the occasional overly-generous gift.

1 Leeds United have appeared in the Charity Shield three times, but on how many of those occasions did we lift the trophy?

2 And can you name the three managers who have led Leeds out in a Charity Shield match?

3   Who were our opponents in the club's first Charity Shield appearance in 1969, and where was the game played?

4   Can you name the striker who made his Leeds debut in the 1969 game?

5   And can you recall the final score in that first Charity Shield appearance?

6   Our other two Charity Shield appearances were both against Liverpool. The first of these encounters took place in 1974 and ended in a 1–1 draw. Who scored our equaliser in that game?

7   The 1974 game was eventually decided by penalties. Can you recall the unlikely penalty taker who missed the decisive sixth spot-kick for Leeds after the first five had all been scored?

8 During the 1974 Charity Shield, an unseemly brawl broke out between two players, resulting in them both being sent from the field. Can you name the fist-flailing duo involved in this infamous clash?

9 In which year did we make our most recent appearance to date in the Charity Shield?

10 And can you name our hat-trick hero that day?

11 Finally, which player came on as a late substitute in that game and scored a classic comedy own goal, neatly back-heeling the ball into his own net after a couple of deft touches?

FIVES AND FOURS

Name the five successful penalty takers in the 1974 Charity Shield match.

Round
30

Marching on
Together

Congratulations, you've made it to the end of the quiz. And
as a final reward for all of your efforts I've saved my hardest
questions on the club's early years for this last round!
Only kidding – I'm actually signing off with a slightly more
frivolous, light-hearted affair. I'm throwing my very own
'end-of-quiz' party and I'm inviting an array of former players
and a few of our club's celebrity supporters. See how many
of these party guests you can identify as we all raise a toast
to Super Leeds United!

I The first thing our final-round party needs is a few
    famous faces, so let's kick off with a couple of celebrity
    fans. Can you name the Australian star of the films
    Gladiator and *A Beautiful Mind* who has been a Leeds fan
    since the 1970s?

2   And do you know the name of the 'magical' Leeds-born actor who escaped Hogwarts to appear on *Soccer AM* in 2012 wearing a Leeds shirt and brandishing a 'Bates Out' poster?

3   Finally on the thespian theme, which hardman British actor, star of numerous films including *Snatch* and *Escape Plan*, has a Leeds badge tattooed on his leg?

4   Right, let's really get this 'end of-quiz' party going now with some music! The Kaiser Chiefs are passionate Leeds United fans, but do you know the origins of the band's name?

5   And I know I might be pushing the musical theme a bit here, but which stuttering pop idol is also a fan of our great club?

6   Now we need a DJ to make our final round go with a swing, so can you name the verbose former Radio 1 presenter who is a well-known Leeds United supporter?

7   All we need now is a smooth operator to get up on the dance floor and start the dancing. So can you name the former Leeds United lothario bought from Man United in 1996, but probably better known these days for his appearances on *Celebrity Love Island* and *Dancing on Ice*?

8 And which former Leeds defender, who appeared on
   Celebrity Masterchef in 2012, might come in handy with
   the buffet?

9 A particular player from the 1980s who delayed his own
   'party' to play for Leeds definitely deserves an invite.
   Can you name the popular defender who played in
   the 1987 FA Cup semi-final when he should have been
   getting married?

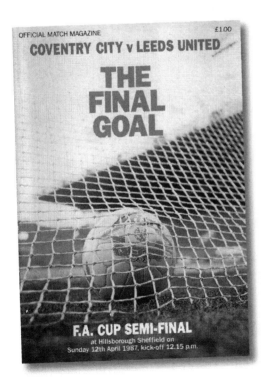

10 This former captain may not be such a universally popular choice, but it wouldn't be a party if someone wasn't arguing and falling out! So can you name the player who scored against Walsall at Elland Road in 1989, but whose frustrated 'hand gesture' to the Kop after scoring saw him subbed, stripped of the captaincy and out of Elland Road before he could say 'But I don't want to go to Bradford City!'?

11 Finally, even virtual parties need a guest of honour and there is only one candidate for me. So, which true Leeds legend, who was voted Footballer of the Year in 1970 with 95 per cent of the vote, had the motto 'Keep Fighting' above his peg?

FACT OR FICTION?

> *In 2008, Lucas Radebe had a beer named after him by the Leeds Brewery Company – Radebeer.*

CHEERS!

THE ANSWERS

Premier
Leeds

1 12.

2 Lee Chapman, who actually scored both goals in that game and ended the season with 13 League goals.

3 Eric Cantona.

4 Mark Viduka, who netted 59 times in 130 Premier League appearances.

5 We became the first team to fail to win an away fixture in the Premier League all season.

6 Gordon Strachan, although Gary McAllister was team captain and actually skippered the team more often than Strachan that season.

7 Dominic Matteo, who was one of the few players to emerge from that dire season with any credit.

8 George Graham, David O'Leary, Terry Venables and Peter Reid.

9 Gary Kelly, who made 531 appearances for us in total, 325 in the Premier League.

10 We finished the season third in the table, although we were actually top as the new millennium dawned.

11 The 4–1 defeat away at Bolton Wanderers condemned us to relegation.

FACT OR FICTION

Fiction – Wetherall actually made 201 Premier League appearances for Leeds, while Woodgate made just 104.

All the Glory
of the Cup

1   1972, and the scorer was, of course, Allan Clarke.
2   Four – all under Don Revie (1965, 1970, 1972 and 1973).
3   Billy Bremner – the tie ended 1–0.
4   Albert Johanneson, a hugely talented player remembered
    with great affection by Leeds United fans. Unfortunately,
    he failed to showcase his talents in the 1965 final, freezing
    in the 2–1 defeat at the hands of Liverpool.
5   Hereford United. The tie needed a replay following a 0–0
    draw at Hereford.
6   Tottenham Hotspur.
7   Not one of our proudest records, but we were knocked out
    of the FA Cup in the third round for 10 consecutive seasons
    between 1952/53 and 1961/62; for three seasons running
    during that period (1955/56, 1956/57 and 1957/58) we were
    defeated 2–1 by the same team,   Cardiff City.
8   Arsenal.
9   Ipswich Town, who finally
    triumphed 3–2 in the third replay.
10 Brendan Ormsby.
11 The 1970 FA Cup final replay
    against Chelsea, which 28.5 million
    people watched. It was one of
    only two sporting events to
    appear in the top 10 (the 1966
    World Cup final topped the table
    with 32.3 million viewers).

FACT OR FICTION

Fiction – We've been drawn against Man United seven times in the FA Cup, although some of those ties were extremely memorable. However, the club that we have faced most often is Arsenal. We have been drawn against the Gunners on nine separate occasions including, most memorably, the final in 1972.

The Boss

1 Revie signed for Leeds United from Sunderland in 1958.

2 The Football Writers' Association Footballer of the Year.

3 Bournemouth. The very thought sends a shudder down the spine – how different the club's history could have been…

4 1961/62.

5 1963/64, unleashing one of the greatest teams of all time into the English First Division.

6 A heartbreaking five times: 1964/65; 1965/66; 1969/70; 1970/71, and 1971/72.

7 Four – three Inter-Cities Fairs Cup finals and one European Cup Winners' Cup final.

8 Four – the League Cup once; the FA Cup once, and the Inter-Cities Fairs Cup twice.

9 Mick Bates.

10 QPR – Revie's final League game as manager was at Loftus Road on 27 April 1974. Leeds, already confirmed Champions, won the game 1–0.

11 Johnny Giles. The board, unfortunately, had other ideas.

FIVES AND FOURS

Billy Bremner, Allan Clarke, Johnny Giles, Norman Hunter and Paul Madeley.

It's all Relative!

PRESS INFORMATION

Coca Cola League Cup Final 24th March 1996 - Kick off 5.00pm
Aston Villa v Leeds United
Wembley Stadium

	ASTON V		LEEDS U
1.	Mark Bosnich	1.	John Lukic
2.	Gary Charles	2.	Gary Kelly
3.	Alan Wright	3.	Lucas Radebe
4.	Gareth Southgate	4.	Carlton Palmer
5.	Paul McGrath	5.	John Pemberton
6.	Ugo Ehiogu	6.	David Wetherall
7.	Ian Taylor	7.	Andy Gray
8.	Mark Draper	8.	Mark Ford
9.	Savo Milosevic	9.	Anthony Yeboah
10.	Dwight Yorke	10.	Gary McAllister (c)
11.	Andy Townsend (c)	11.	Gary Speed
12.	Steve Staunton	12.	Brian Deane
13.	Michael Oakes	13.	Tomas Brolin
14.	Tommy Johnson	14.	Nigel Worthington

Managers: Brian Little   Howard Wilkinson
Colours: Claret & Blue Shirts   All White with Yellow
                White Shorts   and Blue Trim
Referee: Robbie Hart
Linesmen: Brian Coddington and Martin Sims
Reserve Official: Jim Rushton

Eat Football. Sleep Football. Drink Coca-Cola

1   Eddie and Frank Gray.
2   Ian and Glynn Snodin.
3   Brian Greenhoff, whose
    older brother Jimmy was
    playing for Leeds in the final.
4   Andy Gray, whose uncle
    Eddie played in the 1968 final.
5   Gary Kelly and his nephew
    Ian Harte.
6   John Stiles.
7   Jack Charlton.
8   Allan Clarke, whose four
    professional footballing
    brothers were Frank,
    Derek, Kelvin and Wayne.
9   Charlie Keetley, who scored over 100 goals for Leeds
    between 1927 and 1934; his brothers Tom, Frank, Harold
    and Joe also regularly scored for other clubs.
10 Rod and Ray Wallace.
11 Nathan and Lewis Turner.

FACT OR FICTION
Fact –The two brothers were Jack and Bobby Charlton,
who each bagged a goal in the 2–2 draw between Leeds and
Man United in October 1970.

Leeds International

1 Lucas Radebe.
2 Philemon Masinga.
3 Eddie Lewis.
4 Manuel Rui Marques.
5 Mark Viduka.
6 Max Gradel.
7 Tony Yeboah.
8 Olivier Dacourt.
9 Eirik Bakke.
10 Tomas Brolin.
11 Roque Junior.

FIVES AND FOURS

El-Hadji Diouf, Rodolph Austin, Luciano Becchio, Davide
Somma and Habib Habibou.

'White' from the Start

1 1919.
2 Dick Ray, who managed Leeds United during their inaugural season playing in the Midland League.
3 Blue and white stripes for the first fifteen years. When Leeds United was formed following the demise of Leeds City, Huddersfield Town chairman Hilton Crowther proposed the amalgamation of his club with the newly formed Leeds outfit. The merger plans eventually came to nothing but Crowther joined Leeds anyway as chairman of the club – hence the blue and white stripes!
4 The opponents were Port Vale, not too popular in Leeds at the time as they had been vocal in calling for Leeds City's expulsion from the League and then eagerly took their place in the Second Division.
5 Len Armitage, who scored in the 2–1 defeat against South Shields in Leeds United's first home game.
6 John Charles.
7 Willis Edwards.
8 Wilf Copping.
9 Grenville Hair.
10 1923/24, promoted as Second Division Champions.
11 Leeds finished fifth in the First Division in 1929/30.

FACT OR FICTION
Fact – The club's badge originally featured three owls and was based on the City of Leeds coat of arms, while a peacock appeared on the Leeds badge during the early 1980s.

Away Days

1 Southampton. A famous 3–4 victory for Leeds, who came back from 3–0 down, scoring all four goals in the last 20 minutes to complete a spectacular comeback.

2 Hull City. Leeds won the fixture 4–1 and in doing so secured promotion to the First Division.

3 Swansea City. Leeds once again returned to the top flight of football courtesy of a 3–0 victory over the Welshmen.

4 Lazio. The game, in the second group stage of the Champions League, ended in a 1–0 victory to Leeds, with Alan Smith scoring the winner. Leeds, widely tipped to finish bottom of the group, actually finished second behind Real Madrid and progressed to the knockout stage.

5 Colchester United. Leeds, top of Division One, met Fourth Division minnows Colchester in the fifth round of the FA Cup and the underdogs pulled off a major shock, winning 3–2 to despatch us from the Cup.

6 Nottingham Forest. A 4–0 victory to Leeds, on an emotional night following the death of former Elland Road favourite Gary Speed.

7 Leicester City. Leeds United's 6–0 annihilation of Leicester City in the third round of the League Cup remains, to date, our record victory in that competition.

8 Coventry City. Second Division Leeds fought bravely against First Division opponents in the FA Cup semi-final and almost pulled off a glorious shock. Coventry needed extra-time to defeat us 3–2.

9 Barcelona. A 1–1 draw in the European Cup semi-final second leg in Spain earned Leeds a place in the final following a 2–1 home victory in the first leg.

10 Histon. This FA Cup second-round televised clash resulted in a humiliating 1–0 defeat for Leeds, our first ever defeat against non-league opposition.

11 Wimbledon (who shared a ground with Crystal Palace between 1991 and 2002). This memorable 4–2 Leeds victory featured a fabulous Tony Yeboah hat-trick, which included the Goal of the Season.

FIVES AND FOURS

Bloomfield Road, Ewood Park, Reebok Stadium, Turf Moor and City of Manchester Stadium (or Etihad Stadium, if your prefer), the homes of Blackpool, Blackburn Rovers, Bolton Wanderers, Burnley and Manchester City, respectively. The first four were for League fixtures and the latter in the FA Cup.

War of the Roses

1 A 0–0 draw – not, unfortunately, a resounding victory for us!
2 Two; the first and second games, played at Hillsborough and
   Villa Park respectively, both ended goal-less, so a second
   replay at Burnden Park was required, which we finally won
   1–0. The winning goal was scored by Billy Bremner.
3 Jermaine Beckford – who could forget!
4 Brian Flynn.
5 Mick Jones, who scored a total of seven goals.
6 Alan Smith, in the 1–1 draw at Old Trafford in February 2004.
7 Gunnar Halle.
8 Jack Charlton.
9 Paul Reaney.
10 1973/74.
11 We won 3–2 against Sheffield United while Man United
   lost 2–0 at Liverpool.

FACT OR FICTION
Fiction – The club's record attendance is actually 57,892
against Sunderland in a fifth-round FA Cup replay in March 1967.

Name that Player

Player A: Tony Currie.
Player B: Mervyn Day.
Player C: Gordon McQueen.
Player D: Aaron Lennon.
Player E: Tony Dorigo.
Player F: Arthur Graham.

FIVES AND FOURS

Imre Varadi in 1990, Jon
Newsome and David
Wetherall in 1991, and
Carlton Palmer and Nigel
Worthington in 1994. Glynn Snodin was also transferred
directly from Wednesday, but before Wilkinson took over at
Leeds. A whole host of other former Sheffield Wednesday
players also ended up at Elland Road (including Lee Chapman,
John Pearson, Mel Sterland and Carl Shutt), but none of them
were transferred directly from Wednesday.

We was Robbed

1 Peter Lorimer; a thunderous volley on 66 minutes, when the score was still 0–0.
2 Franz Beckenbauer.
3 Michel Kitabdjian, although you can give yourself the point if you said Beckenbauer!
4 AC Milan.
5 Greek – following the final (played in Salonika), referee Christos Michas was banned from football for life – small consolation for Leeds fans.
6 Barcelona.
7 Valencia.
8 West Bromwich Albion. Jeff Astle was the scorer and we lost the game 2–1, and the title by a single point if you needed to be reminded.
9 Ray Tinkler – no doubt regarded as a hero by Arsenal fans that season.
10 Chelsea.
11 Wolves at Molineux.

FACT OR FICTION

Fiction – Somewhat surprisingly, Bremner was never voted Leeds United Player of the Year, although I suppose this anomaly is partly due to the fact that the award was only introduced in 1970/71.

Round 11

It'll be all 'White' on the Night

1 Tom Lees, who equalised for Hull with an own goal but quickly made amends when he scored to put us back ahead before half-time. The game eventually finished with a 4–1 victory.

2 Gary Sprake, who somehow managed to throw the ball backwards into his own net. We lost the game 2–0.

3 Richard Naylor – victory at the Valley would have secured promotion with a game to spare.

4 Max Gradel.

5 Norman Hunter.

6 Tresor Kandol and Jermaine Beckford. Kandol received his marching orders before half-time after being booked twice, first for appealing for a foul, and then for sarcastically applauding the referee when he was awarded a free-kick. Beckford received two yellow cards within 10 minutes of the restart, the first for chipping the goalie after the whistle had been blown, and the second for committing a foul. The game ended in a 1–1 draw, with Gillingham equalising in the first minute of injury time.

7 Richard Cresswell.

8 El Hadji Diouf and Rodolph Austin.

9 Everton, at an extremely hostile Goodison Park.

10 Valencia. Jack Charlton, who had been kicked and punched, lost his head and a mass brawl ensued. The players were taken from the field to calm down but Charlton and one of the Valencia players were told not to return when play eventually resumed – they had both been sent off!

11 Paul Rachubka. The game ended in a dismal 5–0 defeat,
with 18-year-old debutant Alex Cairns replacing Rachubka
for the second half.

FACT OR FICTION
Fiction – Vinnie was actually never sent off while playing for
Leeds and only received three yellow cards throughout that
whole season.

The Last is the First

1 Danny **Mills**.
2 Gary **Speed**.
3 El Hadji **Diouf**.
4 Chris **Fairclough**.
5 Norman **Hunter**.
6 Ian **Rush**.
7 David **Healy**.
8 Terry **Yorath**.
9 Alf-Inge **Haaland**.
10 Jonathan **Douglas**.
11 John **Sheridan**.

FIVES AND FOURS

David Harvey, Billy Bremner, Joe Jordan, Peter Lorimer and Gordon McQueen.

Leeds! Leeds! Leeds!

1 Aidan White.
2 Lloyd Sam.
3 David Batty.
4 Paul Madeley.
5 Noel Whelan.
6 Alan Smith, who blotted his copybook somewhat when he transferred to Man United in 2004.
7 Brian Deane.
8 David Harvey.
9 James Milner.
10 Mike O'Grady.
11 Aidan Butterworth.

FACT OR FICTION
Fiction – Paul Reaney was actually born in Fulham, although he did grow up in Leeds after his family moved to the city when he was a baby.

Hot
Shots

1 Peter Lorimer, who scored 168 League goals in his two spells at the club between 1962–79 and 1983–85.
2 John Charles, who scored 42 League goals in Division Two during the 1953/54 season.
3 Tom Jennings, although ironically his efforts couldn't prevent Leeds being relegated at the end of the season.
4 Mick Jones, in the 5–1 win at Elland Road in February 1972.
5 Captain Jonny Howson. His first goal came when the score was 1–1. We went on to win 4–1.

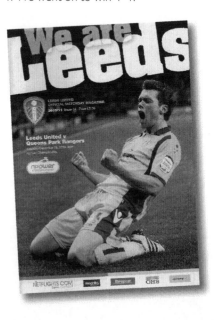

6 Lee Chapman. Leeds were 4–0 down at half-time, but Chapman's hat-trick and a Carl Shutt goal restored our pride, even though the game eventually ended in a 4–5 defeat.

7 Mark Viduka.

8 Allan Clarke.

9 Jermaine Beckford, who scored 34 goals in all competitions.

10 Tony Yeboah.

11 Jimmy Floyd Hasselbaink, who shared the award with Michael Owen and Dwight Yorke when he scored 18 goals in 36 appearances that season. The Dutch striker remains the only Leeds player to have won this award.

FACT OR FICTION

Fact – Despite leaving the club in the January transfer window, the Argentine's tally of 19 goals was enough for him to remain the club's leading goalscorer that season.

Super Stoppers

1 John Lukic.
2 Gary Sprake. The 16-year-old was rushed from Leeds by taxi and chartered aircraft when Tommy Younger was taken ill; kick-off was delayed to give him time to arrive!
3 Paul Robinson.
4 Casper Ankergren.
5 Kasper Schmeichel.
6 Nigel Martyn, who was 35 years, 289 days old when he played in his last England game – a friendly against Cameroon in May 2002.
7 Neil Sullivan.
8 Paddy Kenny, who had previously played under Warnock at Bury, Sheffield United and QPR.
9 David Seaman.
10 David Stewart.
11 Lucas Radebe, who began his career in South Africa as a goalkeeper. He performed spectacularly between the sticks, keeping a clean sheet while he was in goal against Middlesbrough and conceding just one goal late in the game against Man United.

FIVES AND FOURS
Gary Sprake (506), David Harvey (446), John Lukic (430), Nigel Martyn (273) and Mervyn Day (268).

Three Lions on a Shirt

1 Alan Smith – and this was his only goal for the England senior team.
2 Trevor Cherry, who captained the England national team in his penultimate international appearance.
3 Norman Hunter.
4 Jimmy Armfield.
5 Allan Clarke, who scored the only goal of the game (a penalty) against Czechoslovakia. The striker remains the last England player to make his international debut at the World Cup finals.
6 Terry Cooper.
7 Paul Reaney.
8 Nigel Martyn.
9 Trevor Cherry.
10 Don Revie, Terry Venables and Howard Wilkinson (although Wilkinson was only in a caretaker capacity).
11 Carlton Palmer, Steve Hodge and Michael Ricketts.

FACT OR FICTION
Fiction – Elland Road did stage matches during Euro 96, but has also hosted two full England internationals (a 3–3 draw against Sweden in June 1995, and a 2–1 defeat to Italy in March 2002).

What's in a Name?

1 Peter Lorimer.
2 Mel Sterland.
3 Albert Johanneson.
4 Kevin Hird.
5 John Charles.
6 Joe Jordan.
7 John Pearson.
8 Robert Molenaar.
9 Alan Smith.
10 Jack Charlton.
11 Lucas Radebe.

FIVES AND FOURS
Gordon McQueen in 1975 and 1977, Paul Madeley in 1976, Gary McAllister in 1994 and Nigel Martyn in 1997.

We've had our Ups and Downs...

1 Twice. Relegated in 1926/27 and promoted in 1927/28; then relegated again in 1930/31 and promoted in 1931/32.
2 Newcastle United. We won the game 3–0.
3 Bobby Collins.
4 The Hawthorns.
5 Charlton Athletic.
6 Bournemouth.
7 2003/04.
8 Kevin Blackwell.
9 Ipswich Town. A 1–1 draw made relegation, with one game to go, almost certain.
10 A 1–0 defeat.
11 Jermaine Beckford.

FACT OR FICTION

Fiction – Of the 87 seasons that we have spent in the Football (or Premier) League (1920/21 to 2013/14), 50 have been in the top flight, 34 in the second tier and 3 in the third.

The 'Other' Cup

1 Just once, the season we won it
(1967/68).
2 Arsenal.
3 Terry Cooper, who
volleyed the ball in from an
Eddie Gray corner.
4 Aston Villa.
5 Birmingham City, defeated
5–1 on aggregate.
6 Tony Yeboah.
7 Manchester United, who
won 2–1 in the first leg
at Old Trafford and then
stole a last-minute goal to
triumph 1–0 at Elland Road.
8 Chester City.
9 Everton and Southampton.
10 Chelsea.
11 Don Revie scored the first Leeds goal in the 3–1 replay
victory over Blackpool in the tournament's inaugural year.

FIVES AND FOURS
Peter Lorimer (19 goals), Gary Speed (11 goals), Lee Chapman
(10 goals) and Rod Wallace (8 goals).

White Hot Debuts

1 Luke Varney and David Norris.
2 Rob Hulse.
3 Alan Curtis.
4 Carl Harris.
5 Tommy Wright.
6 Andy Ritchie.
7 Carl Shutt.
8 Frank Strandli.
9 Jimmy-Floyd Hasselbaink.
10 Bobby Davison.
11 Derek Parlane.

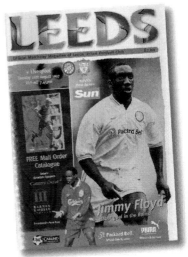

FACT OR FICTION

Fiction – Although Johanneson was one of the first high-profile black men to appear in English top-flight football, the club's first black player was actually his South African compatriot Gerry Francis, a right-winger who made his Leeds debut in 1959.

Connect Four

Connect I

1 Bobby Collins.
2 Gordon Strachan.
3 Billy Bremner.
4 Jack Charlton.

Connection I – They are the four players from Leeds United who have been named the FWA (Football Writers' Association) Footballer of the Year – Collins won the coveted award in 1965; Charlton in 1967; Bremner in 1970, and Strachan in 1991.

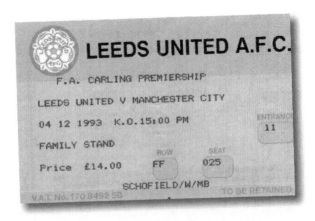

Connect 2

1 Mick Jones.
2 Peter Barnes.
3 Michael Bridges.
4 Rio Ferdinand.

Connection 2 – These four players all arrived at Elland Road for what was, at the time, a club record transfer fee – Jones was signed from Sheffield United for £100,000 in 1967; Barnes moved from West Bromwich Albion for £930,000 in 1981; Bridges joined for £5 million from Sunderland in 1999, and Ferdinand was an £18 million purchase from West Ham United in 2000.

Connect 3

1 David Batty.
2 Ian Baird.
3 Scott Sellars.
4 Frank Gray.

Connection 3 – All four players enjoyed two spells with Leeds United during their professional footballing careers: Batty 1986–1993 and 1998–2004; Baird 1985–1987 and 1988–1990; Sellars 1983–1986 and 1992–1993; and Gray 1972–1979 and 1981–1985.

Connect 4

1 Robert Snodgrass.
2 Jonny Howson.
3 Bradley Johnson.
4 Luciano Becchio.

Connection 4 – All four players have trodden the now well-worn path that leads from Elland Road to Norwich – Johnson moved to Carrow Road in July 2011; Howson in January 2012; Snodgrass in July 2012, and Becchio in January 2013.

FIVES AND FOURS

Ian Harte, Gary Kelly, Harry Kewell and Nigel Martyn.

Sergeant Wilko's
Barmy Army

1 Billy Bremner, although another former Leeds legend,
Norman Hunter, had been in charge on a temporary basis for
the preceding 3 games, which had all ended in defeat.

2 Barnsley, who won the game 2–1.

3 Sheffield United finished runners-up on goal difference;
Newcastle United finished third and missed out
on promotion.

4 Ian Baird, whose goals in the 4–1 victory, along with other
results, consigned Newcastle to another season in the
Second Division while   also ensuring Middlesbrough
avoided relegation.
The striker had
also made enough
appearances for
Leeds before his
departure to pick up
a Second Division
Championship
winners' medal!

5 Gordon Strachan.

6 Everton.

7 Vinnie Jones.
Ironically, we were
Bramall Lane's first
visitors after Vinnie's
transfer.

8 John Lukic and Gary McAllister.
9 We didn't lose at Elland Road all season in a League
   fixture, and lost just 4 League games on our travels.
10 Sheffield Wednesday.
11 Lee Chapman.

FACT OR FICTION

Fact – And he's likely to remain so for the foreseeable future!

The Price is 'White'

1 Rio Ferdinand.
2 Lee Bowyer.
3 Johnny Giles.
4 Eric Cantona.
5 David White signed for Leeds in exchange for David Rocastle.
6 Terry Connor.
7 John McGovern and John O'Hare.
8 Duncan McKenzie – his signing was arguably the only good thing to come from Brian Clough's brief Elland Road reign!
9 Cardiff City.
10 Aston Villa.
11 Derby County.

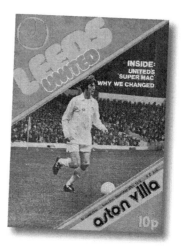

FIVES AND FOURS

Jamie Ashdown, David Norris, Jason Pearce and Luke Varney.

The Life and Times of Leeds United

1 Allan Clarke.
2 Dominic Matteo.
3 Duncan McKenzie.
4 Paul Madeley.
5 Don Revie.
6 Mel Sterland.
7 Joe Jordan.
8 Gary Sprake.
9 Frank Worthington.
10 Terry Yorath.
11 Chris Kamara.
12 Norman Hunter.
13 David O'Leary.
14 John Charles.
15 Gordon Strachan.

FACT OR FICTION

Fiction – Although I'm sure Snodgrass will one day publish his memoirs, he has so far resisted the temptation. *Snod This for a Laugh* is actually the autobiography of former Leeds midfielder Ian Snodin.

We are the Champions, Champions of Europe!

1 Our European debut came in the 1965/66 Inter-Cities Fairs Cup; a 2–1 victory over Torino at Elland Road.
2 Billy Bremner scored the opener in the game against Torino at Elland Road; Alan Peacock added a second.
3 Hajduk Split; Allan Clarke scored the only goal of the tie.
4 Lyn Oslo.
5 We progressed through to the second round following a play-off at the Nou Camp ordered by UEFA after Stuttgart fielded too many foreign players in the second leg.
6 Carl Shutt, who came on as a sub when the score was 1–1 and clinched victory with virtually his first touch.
7 Rod Belfitt.
8 Alan Smith.

9 Peter Lorimer.

10 Norman Hunter.

11 Malaga. The 2–1 home defeat in the third round of the UEFA Cup was our last appearance to date in European competitions. Eirik Bakke scored our only goal that night, so has the distinction of being the last Leeds player to score a goal in Europe.

FIVES AND FOURS

Barcelona, Real Madrid, Deportivo la Coruna and Valencia.

1 Arthur Fairclough, who took over from Dick Ray when the club was elected to the Second Division in 1920.

2 Major Frank Buckley.

3 Eddie Gray, 1982–85 and caretaker in 2003–04.

4 Gary McAllister, who captained Leeds in both the 1992 Charity Shield and 1996 League Cup and led the team out as manager in the woeful 2008 play-off final against Doncaster Rovers.

5 Dennis Wise, in the 2006/07 season.

6 Simon Grayson.

7 Just a single win from 8 games.

8 Jock Stein, who left to become Scotland manager.

9 Johnny Giles and Jack Charlton.

10 Terry Yorath and Gary Speed (although Brian Flynn has also managed Wales in a caretaker capacity).

11 Howard Wilkinson.

FACT OR FICTION

Fact – David O'Leary, the only manager with non-British nationality, was actually born in Stoke Newington, London; all the rest were born in England or Scotland.

Round 27

Who Scored the Goal?

1 Rod Wallace – a mazy run from deep inside his own half, which ended with a curling shot into the top corner that deservedly won many plaudits, including *Match of the Day*'s Goal of the Season for 1993/94.

2 Eddie Gray – take your pick from his two goals! The deft chip from 40 yards that floated over the keeper's head was fantastic, but for me the mesmerising dribble round half the Burnley team was simply sublime.

3 Keith Edwards – vital away goal in the dying seconds of normal time, which levelled the aggregate scores and set up extra time that we then only needed to survive to progress to the play-off final.

4 Bradley Johnson – a stunning long-range strike which nestled in the top-left corner of the Arsenal goal and was rewarded with the club's Goal of the Season award in 2010/11.

5 Gordon Strachan – a sweet strike from the edge of the box near the end of our final home game of the season, which secured the points and kept us firmly in the box-seat for promotion back to the top tier.

6 Tony Yeboah – a truly magnificent volley from 30 yards that dipped and hit the underside of the bar before going into the net; would have won Goal of the Season but for another effort from the Ghanaian in the same campaign!

7 Ross McCormack – a superb curling shot that bent into the top corner of the goal to send Spurs out of the Cup and scoop the Leeds 2012/13 Goal of the Season award for the Scot.

8 David Batty – swept in a cross from the edge of the six-yard box to score his first goal in four years and send Elland Road delirious.

9 Dominic Matteo – famous header that ensured our progression from the first group stage of the 2000/01 Champions League campaign at the expense of our illustrious Italian opponents.

10 Billy Bremner – spectacular overhead kick from a Jack Charlton flick down towards the end of the game that secured a draw against our old rivals.

11 Vinnie Jones – my personal favourite; an absolutely stunning 30-yard volley from the Leeds hardman in an exciting game that simply had everything, including a Leeds injury time winner!

FIVES AND FOURS

Ray Hankin in 1977/78, John Hawley in 1978/79, Kevin Hird in 1979/80 and Carl Harris in 1980/81.

The Kids are all 'White'

1 Peter Lorimer, who made his debut against Southampton at the age of 15 years, 289 days.
2 James Milner, who was 16 years, 356 days at the time; the record has since been broken by Everton's James Vaughan.
3 Jonathan Woodgate, when he played against Bulgaria in June 1999 aged 19 years, 138 days.
4 Gary Sprake, who was 18 years old when he made his full international debut.
5 Harry Kewell.
6 Fabian Delph.
7 Sam Byram.
8 Man United, whose team included David Beckham, Paul Scholes, Gary Neville, Phil Neville, Nicky Butt, Keith Gillespie and Robbie Savage, but they were still no match for our youngsters!
9 Jamie Forrester.
10 Paul Robinson.
11 Danny Rose.

FACT OR FICTION
Fact – Sometimes the truth is stranger than fiction after all!

Sweet Charity

1 Two.
2 Don Revie, Brian Clough and Howard Wilkinson.
3 Man City; and the game was played at Elland Road.
4 Allan Clarke, who had just been signed from Leicester for a British record transfer fee of £165,000.
5 Leeds won 2–1; Eddie Gray and Jack Charlton scored.
6 Trevor Cherry.
7 David Harvey.
8 Billy Bremner and Kevin Keegan.
The pair became the first British players to be sent off at Wembley.
9 1992.
10 Eric Cantona.
11 Gordon Strachan.

FIVES AND FOURS
Peter Lorimer, Johnny Giles, Eddie Gray, Norman Hunter and Trevor Cherry.

Marching on Together

1 Russell Crowe.
2 Matthew Lewis (but if you said 'Neville Longbottom from the Harry Potter films' you can have the point!).
3 Vinnie Jones.
4 They named themselves after the team Lucas Radebe played for in South Africa.
5 Gareth Gates.
6 Chris Moyles.
7 Lee Sharpe.
8 Danny Mills.
9 Neil Aspin.
10 Mark Aizlewood.
11 Billy Bremner.

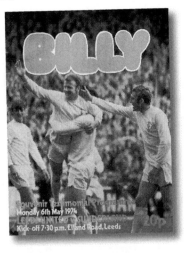

FACT OR FICTION

Fact – In 2008 the Leeds Brewery ran a competition amongst Leeds United fans to name its new brew, and Radebeer pipped Billy's Pride to come out on top! From every pint sold 10p was donated to the Leeds United transfer fund.

38429344R00081

Printed in Great Britain
by Amazon